The Lighter Side of
Campus Life

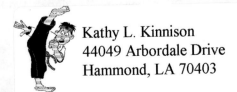

Campus Life Books

Against All Odds
Alive
Alive II
The Campus Life Guide to Dating
The Campus Life Guide to Making and Keeping Friends
The Campus Life Guide to Surviving High School
The Life of the Party
The Lighter Side of Campus Life
A Love Story
Peer Pressure: Making It Work for You
What Teenagers Are Saying About Drugs and Alcohol
Worth the Wait
You Call This a Family?

The Lighter Side of
Campus Life

A DIVISION OF CTI
CampusLife / **Z**
BOOKS / Zondervan Publishing House
Grand Rapids, Michigan

The Lighter Side of Campus Life
Copyright © 1986, 1990 by Campus Life
All rights reserved

Published by Zondervan Publishing House
1415 Lake Drive, S.E., Grand Rapids, Michigan 49506

Library of Congress Cataloging-in-Publication Data

The Lighter side of Campus life.
    p. cm.
    Cartoon collection from Campus Life magazine.
    Reprint. Originally published: Wheaton, Ill. : Tyndale House,
1989.
    ISBN 0-310-71061-8
    1. College students—Caricatures and cartoons. 2. College
teachers—Caricatures and cartoons. 3. American wit and humor,
Pictorial. 4. Campus life (Wheaton, Ill.) I. Campus Life
Wheaton, Ill.)
NC1428.C26 1990
741.5′9773′24—dc20

                                                    90–34439
                                                      CIP

Printed in the United States of America

90 91 92 93 94 / CH / 5 4 3 2 1

Summer Vacation

AAHHH, this is the life. No mid-terms, no classes, no book reports, no studying, no report cards, no finals . . .

Let's find another spot.
These Frisbees are blocking out the sun.

Sorry . . . it's the only way I can cover tuition costs.

That's it . . . 657,984 boards! Now let's count 'em again to make sure.

Very well, then, will the real
summer camp counselor please stand up?

Bored to tears? Break the routine with a little Strange Behavior.

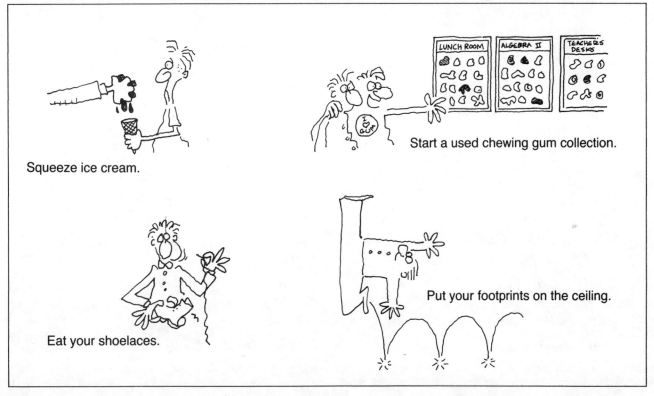

Squeeze ice cream.

Start a used chewing gum collection.

Eat your shoelaces.

Put your footprints on the ceiling.

Beat the Blahs

Wear the wrong size clothes.

Wear more shoes.

Feel people's smiles.

Stick celery in your ears.

Beat the Blahs

Back to School

Getting desperate, aren't they?

Seniors!

Uh, oh, looks like they're taking
a tougher disciplinary stand this year.

Why do they always do that on the first day of school? They just saw each other yesterday!

Back again for the fifth time to throw out the ceremonial first spitball, officially opening the '85-86 season is our very own Bubba Cassidy.

Yes, I'm sure Advanced Calculus and Principles/
Theories of Nuclear Physics will impress
Mary Ann Compton, but, if I may be so bold,
I'd suggest perhaps a short course in
basic mathematics first?

We still have a few bugs to work out
in our locker assignment system.

I guess this must be homeroom.

Tried-and-True Ways to Beat the Back-to-School Blahs

Pretend you are a mannequin.

Eat your lunch through a straw.

See how many pencils
you can stick in your hair.

Do your homework with your feet.

Wear a disguise.

Beg your teachers for more homework.

Never take off your gym socks.

Count the gum wads
under your desk.

Catch your finger
in your notebook ring.

Free all the science lab animals.

Excuse me, sir . . . I'm afraid I'll have to ask that you read more quietly to yourself

Peter, I sure wish I was as popular
as you think you are.

I see that you guessed wrong on 50 percent of the test questions. . . . You might want to consider becoming a weatherman.

Lunchtime

You don't understand. I don't mean it's the same stuff we had
the last day of school last year. I mean it's the *same* stuff!

Look, everybody! A well-balanced meal!

Pepperoni pizza, potato salad, grape Kool-Aid, Jell-O. Oh, no! That's what I had for breakfast!

I hate it when we have spaghetti!

They're mashed potatoes . . . one lump or two?

Nah, it's liver and Brussels sprouts
. . . turns out it's just his nickname.

"FOOD FIGHT!"

Be careful, I sat next to Tubby Thompson
one time and he ate my algebra book.

They probably only mean the paper products.

Now I'm really starved!
I only had 15 minutes for lunch
and the monitor gave me
a 10-minute lecture on scarfing my food.

Student Elections

. . . The good news is we've rounded up 50 supporters for you. The bad news is 43 go to another school.

I give you a student who doesn't know
the meaning of the word "surrender" . . .
who doesn't know the meaning of the word
"compromise" . . . who doesn't know the meaning
of lots of other words, either . . .

Getting a tad overdramatic, aren't we, Willard?

Stop at every telephone pole.

Mister Principal! We, the members of Lake Brantley High, Class of '85, ever mindful of our responsibility for good citizenship, cast 18 votes for Dale Colangelo, 23 votes for Ellen Parkinson and 187 votes for Jacques Cousteau Clarke, who promises Perrier water in all drinking fountains.

This might alter our campaign strategy
a bit, Dink . . .

Please vote for me for secretary-treasurer.
I can write and I like money. Thank you.

My, my! I do believe
"election-eve-panic" is setting in.

Ah, ah, ah, Bubba! You know the rules . . .
no electioneering within 50 feet of the polling place!

Biology

That was a stroke of genius, Sally! I think naming them Mickey and Kermit may have just saved their lives.

This mutually beneficial relationship between plants and people can, however, be a bit misleading. Take, for instance, that poison ivy you're holding.

Now *that* puts things in a new light!
Instead of being fat, I just
have an over-developed cell structure.

Notice also the contraction of the frog's leg muscle
and the spasmodic reflexes of the lower . . .

Nice going, Mom!
You just smashed my insect project,
along with any hopes I might've had
of passing biology.

But there *are* 20 leaves, Ma'am! Nineteen varieties
mounted on, if I may point out, a table leaf.

Industrial Arts

Hold it steady.

We'd rather you didn't play with the tools, Bubba.

I must admit, at first I figured they were
overly ambitious, it being
their first project and all.

Very nice, Brantley. But not quite
what we mean by Industrial Art.

I *finally* figured out how I could make
an A in Industrial Arts.

A PLACE FOR
EVERYTHING
AND
EVERYTHING
IN ITS PLACE

Oh, no, not just a toothpick, sir.
This is a hand-crafted,
solid walnut, residual nourishment remover.

Excuse me, sir. Did you say B-minus?

Oh? Then I assume you're not familiar with the nesting preferences of the top-sided, slope-headed, pigeon-toed sapsucker.

Safety is one thing, Remley,
but if the truth be known, you're just plain scared, aren't you?

Very good, Johnny. Now, for your next science project, how about disarming it?

Physical Education

Believe me, girls, by the end of the semester
you'll be in as good a shape as I am.

Let's approach this logically:
Don't you need at least one physically
unfit person to compare
the others' progress to?

Here he comes with his old "I lost my contact lenses and couldn't see where I was running" routine again.

A Day in Driver's Ed

Now, with a firm but steady pressure,
gradually apply the brake. . . !

Put it between the two cones.

Check.

There! Right on the ol' button!

No, the "dumb cow" is not in our road.
We, Maryann, we are in its pasture!

Okay, you can give this stuff a try.
Dissolves rust and corrosion, loosens frozen bolts.
I mean, you gotta pry his fingers off there somehow!

Now wait a minute! You said, "Before pulling out into traffic, check the rear-view mirror." I did and it was there!

Out there? Are you insane? We can't go out there!
That's a street!

Can you believe that?
A lousy D in "road attitude"
just because I said the turn signal
had a good beat to it!

Sports

Did you hear that, Charley?
He's a freshman . . . pinch me!

Look, I know it's confusing coming right from football into basketball, but here we don't run out of bounds with the ball to stop the clock.

THE PUCK STOPS HERE

Over the obstacle, Copeland, *over* the obstacle!

I don't think I made the cross-country team.
I asked Coach Gibson which countries
we were going to run across
and he told me to go home.

He just says it makes him feel good.

It's the same old story. Girl meets boy, girl completely destroys boy
with her topspin lobs, girl loses boy.

Run out to right field and tell Smertneck
to look alive out there!

This makes thirty games
without changing my lucky socks!

Which brings us to the rather obvious question. Why do they call this a softball?

See if you can tear off a little piece
of one of their uniforms so he can get the scent.

I wish that I could make
the varsity basketball team this year.

No, no, no! Not among yourselves!

Not just a good tackle by Bronsky—a great tackle!

Go in for Glutsky, Smith, and Barnes.

OK, we've pushed 'em back,
pushed 'em back, w-a-a-y back. Now what?

When I said, "Go in there and get that quarterback,"
I didn't mean bring him over here.

And about that time they decided to de-emphasize football.

Parents

Make a fuss. This is the coffee
Susan's Home Ec class made today.

Dad saw your report card.

I'd like to have the car tonight, Dad, and I'd rather not use force.

Never mind about water conservation . . . go wash the car!

If your father earns $21,000 a year,
how much more will he have to earn if you
go to an exclusive college
with an unlimited expense account and your own car?

Because I've got
three teenagers, that's why.

It's no use, Mom . . . we're not communicating.

We had it installed for Steve;
he was always missing the school bus.

Think I should ask Dad for
money to buy a new oil filter?

Charles, don't buy your mother
any more books about aerobic cooking.

Don't bother your dad now—he just missed
one million dollars in the state lottery by one number.

Before I show you my report card, might we discuss
the possibility of a reduced sentence
with an option for parole?

Christmas

Do you have one that says,
"You're my dearest friend
in the whole world and always will be.
P.S. Keep your catty claws
off my boyfriend!". . . ?

I don't think Mrs. Moorby was too thrilled about getting snowballed at the end of "Silent Night."
Somebody better tell Bubba that Christmas caroling isn't the same as trick-or-treating.

Slaving through this math,
Gets really tough these days,
If the teacher had a heart,
Then he'd give us all A's! Oh,
Jingle Bells, teacher's swell . . .

Not quite so close together.

Merry Christmas, Vicki!
The stores were out of your sizes
so I'm going to let you date Tim until January.

Thank you, Jay, but sometimes it *is* the gift
that counts, not just the thought!

Last one. I wonder what the odds are
that you somehow stuffed a Corvette in here?

So help me, the next person who says,
"So long, Marcie, see you next year!"
is in for a facelift with a snowball!

Romance

I always bring Pookey on the first date!

Hey, Jennifer! "Better-than-nobody" is here!

Of course we're still going steady, Rodney! It's just that you're going a bit steadier than I am!

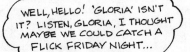

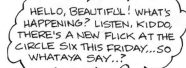

Duane, do I have bad breath
or something?

Now, Alice, let's get this straight.
If Mark calls, you're here; if Dale calls,
you're out; if Bill calls, you'll see him tomorrow;
if Dan calls . . ."

Your daughter tells me you're loaded . . .

This is really nice, Boomer, but couldn't I just wear your class ring?

We interrupt our regularly scheduled classwork for this special report: "Angel-face: Pooh Bear will meet you at Ecstasy Arch after school. His heart is hammering in anticipation of being with you again. . . . He reaffirms his undying love. . ."

I've heard some people say Cynthia is a bit *too* honest.

Fasten your seat belt or you'll keep sliding off the seat.

My daughter's allergic to roses,
but I'm not . . . thank you.

Maybe the young lady would like to order while you gasp.

Be patient . . . just one more after this.

Well . . . Did he ask you or didn't he?

Rest assured, sir, this is only our menu
. . . you and your date will not be quizzed on it later.

First the good news.
Both girls waiting for you
in the lobby, expecting a meal
and a movie, are beautiful. . . .

Our relationship lacks mutual interests.
I like bowling, Oriental food and jazz,
and he likes Connie Laskin.

You'll have my answer in a moment.

Usually I walk Mary Ann to her
third-hour class after P.E.,
but lately she's been ignoring me.
Do you suppose it's the toothpaste
I've been using?

Goodnight, Randy. It's been
a once-in-a-lifetime experience, I hope!

See you tomorrow!

I tell you, that's the last time I go
roller skating with a football player!

Dad likes me in on time.

Loreen, your computer date is here!

But, Gloria, we're not finished. . . .
I haven't said *my* "I do."

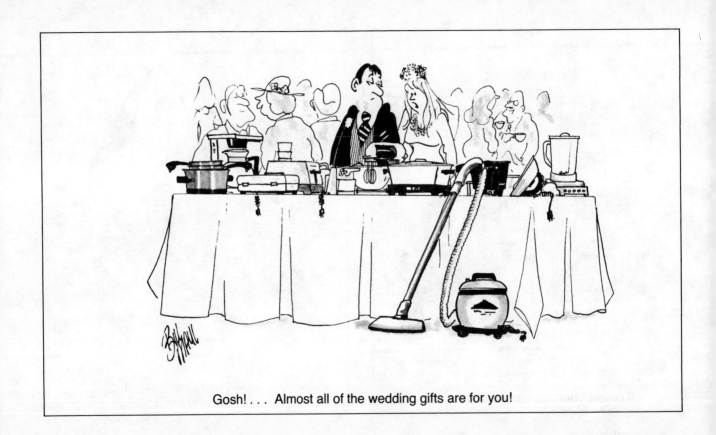

Gosh! . . . Almost all of the wedding gifts are for you!

Hey! Who put this "Under New Management" bumper sticker on my car?

Graduation

Wake up, Dennis. High school's over.

The Class of '83 left a flagpole. The Class of '84 left a bank of trees. And our class, the respectable Class of '85, would like to just *leave*.

Goodbye, little cobweb; goodbye, gym socks; goodbye, little dustballs; goodbye, chewing gum wrappers; goodbye . . .

Guess they meant it when they said, "Absolutely no one will graduate until all overdue books and fines are in!"

Football players.

That's it, big smiles now!
Just think, no more school . . .

. . . no more classes,
no more dumb school plays . . .

. . . no more lousy cafeteria, no more pep rallies,
no more . . .

Jobs

It's my first job, Judy, but there's absolutely nothing to this babysitting.

Imagine my surprise when I found out *bus* boy
wasn't an abbreviation for *business* boy!
But I've decided to keep the job
until an internship opens up in management.

It's not that I don't respect your mother's opinion,
but do you have any other references?

Heavy date?! Did I say *heavy date?!*
Oh, no sir, I meant . . . *meditate*. . . . Yeah, that's it!
I'd like Saturday night off because I've gotta *meditate*.

Why, of course, there's room for
advancement. You certainly can't
go *down* from here!

. . . and I would just like to remind you, Miss Wiley, that here at Madison, Humphrey & Burns we prefer to think of your position as "assistant sanitation technician," not as "toilet trainee."

Honor student to assist National Director of Research and Planning for an international engineering conglomerate. Must analyze and interpret technical data. Long hours. Provide own transportation. Minimum 85 wpm typing. Familiarity with systems analysis desirable. Willing to relocate. . . . Minimum wage.

Could you please reserve your editorial comments and just stock the shelves?

I'm sorry, young man,
but we need someone who can
read music rather than play by ear.

Fast service? . . .
Naw, they just try to give you that impression.

OK, Alice, this is our last problem. If five people working three grills can fry 600 hamburgers in 2½ hours, how many hamburgers can two people fry on two grills in one hour and 15 minutes?

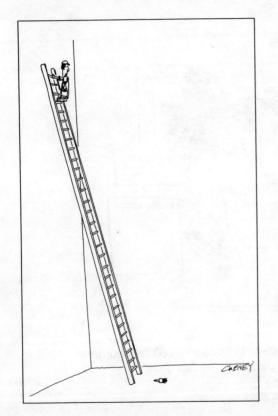

Stop the presses!

How do you feel about
accepting a temporary position?

That was probably where
we were supposed to put it.

I think you should take this one
because I'm freezing.

How many times must I tell you?
Keep the thermostat set at 68!

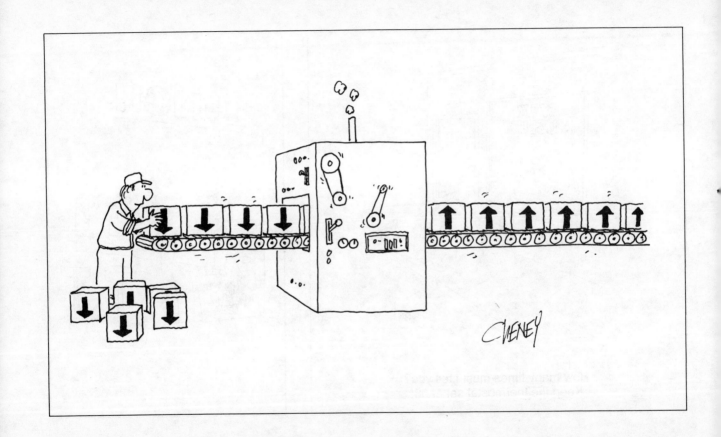